Old Woman by the Sea

by

Doris Kovach

DORRANCE PUBLISHING CO., INC.
PITTSBURGH, PENNSYLVANIA 15222

ISBN: 978-1-4349-0197-2
Library of Congress Control Number: 2008937967

Printed in the United States of America

First Printing

For more information or to order additional books, please contact:
Dorrance Publishing Co., Inc.
701 Smithfield Street
Pittsburgh, Pennsylvania 15222
U.S.A.
1-800-788-7654
www.dorrancebookstore.com

Contents

the beach

observations and thoughts

occurrences

emotions

Sappho's influence

latter day drivel

perhaps loving butterflies…dragonflies…
and the geckos flitting on my path…
the mockingbird's song…the osprey's cry…
the fragrance of jasmine…the morning's sky…
a guitar's lovely melodies…perhaps loving these…
perhaps I do this loving…well….

the beach

The earliest memory I have of life is that of being at a beach, I have always assumed, on the coast of California. I was born in California, in a small, small town up in the Sierra Nevadas, so this beach could have been on the California coast somewhere.

I remember how blue the ocean was. And the waves were rolling into the shore. Not roaring in, but with enough force to curl over with whitecaps in a wash of bubbles and foam, and even for my young eyes: beautiful.

I had to have been at least one year old, because I had walked down toward the water's edge. But having gotten halfway there, I heard behind me to my right my mother calling me to come back. And very soon thereafter, my father was at my left side, taking my hand, turning me around to my left, and leading me back to the blanket where my mother was.

End of memory, but a few magic moments that have affected my life: the beauty of the sea, I remember it still. It is with me always.

The Sea *

Grand,
That's what it is,
Consistent…
Powerful…
It roars and dances,
Falling…dashing…moving…

Tremendously,
It crashes against the rocks,
Lapping…cutting…
Tearing at them.
Never tiring.
Cruel…yet…

Caressingly,
The undertow
Ripples patterns in the sand,
Pulling…
Oh so gently…
That no one would know…
But the grains of sand…

Tiny shells,
Unable to fight,
Willingly
Scatter themselves
From shore…to shore…
Unceasingly…
Over and over,
Relentlessly…the story again.
Children in the sand,
Wind…rain…sun…
From then…'til always…
The sea.

* This is the first poem I ever wrote, after my first visit to Florida. I was sixteen

The Dead Osprey

It lies on the vacant beach
On its back, unnaturally,
Its head buried in the sand
Brought in by the night's tide…
Grace of the sea.

Once resplendent feathers,
Iridescent aerial agility,
Now dull,
Flutter aimlessly…lifelessly…
in Morning's breeze.

Gone the sharp cry.
Blind the keen eye.
The delight, the joy
Of flight, no more.
Pray…life, and all gifts
Were known.
Pray…delight was shown,
Delight of all.

Small flies
Scurry and flit
Around, over the
Still body,
Performing their function
In the life/death pageantry
That surrounds, pervades…
Solemn and still
But for a faint, occasional buzz,
And the eternal lap of waves
Promising peace.

Shadows

On the vast white sands of the morning beach
A little child has found the delight of discovery:
Her shadow,
Which walks when she walks,
Jumps when she jumps,
And dances with her in glee,
Ever there, ever faithful.

Her mother, in radiance, smiles
In the joy discovery has brought,
And the two abandon themselves
To fun…
Chase and tag fleeting images of themselves,
Laughter like merry bells, flutters as butterfly wings,
Gay, innocent abandonment of
All but this moment
And the wonder and magic of themselves.

But how precious…how fragile…
For a cloud soon covers the sun,
While hundreds of miles away
The spectre of Columbine
Spreads its shadow across the land,
And innocence is lost to all.

The laid-back gull of Fort Myers Beach,
Not a Royal Tern, nervously excited,
Not a, Laughing Gull
Laughing at his own speech,
But a plain ol', same ol',
No need to hide it,
Garbage…picking…gull!

He strolls the beach in bedraggled array,
Feathers tied back in a ponytail.
He sizes you up, struts and says,
"I see you, and
You see me, and
If you let me do my thing, why
I'll…let you do yours. But

I would like a bite of your sandwich,
Maybe two,
And those chips you're having with your brew,
You don't have to tough it
Out on your own.
My friend,
I'll gladly help you.

No!…Well,…you don't need
To tell me to stuff it.
Later then."
And sauntering away without concern,
Far too casual to be a tern,
Perhaps he's just heard
Too much Jimmy Buffet.

Sauter de Joie

Late day,
Lagoon's flat, murky green, shiny surface,
Reflects the sky's blue in a few ripples.
Warm, so warm, and still.
Birds all gone elsewhere.
Alone, and peaceful.
Heat haze, shimmering surface.
Bugs here and there penetrate causing
Expanding concentric circles
Swayed by subsurface currents.

Then the ballet begins,
So fast, the eye almost misses
The missile shape from below,
Breaks through the surface, and
Leaps into the air above,
In a spray of scintillating droplets,
To fall back splashing.
But this is not all.
Again, and again, and again, and again
It leaps
In a semi-circular crescent of delight.

Was it just the bugs?
Or clearing the gills?
Oh no..... it was much more!

Morning Mantra

Twenty billion years our Earth has been.
Twenty thousand years our present maze.
I walk the beach, my morning regimen.
At water's edge it sits in final gaze.

A bird, my nearness, instincts now ignore.
Instead the sea controls its identity.
While life surrounds, its rightness does implore,
The bird, in grace, accepts inevitability.

Would that I may show such final grace.
And turning to follow my footprints in the sand,
I'm awed by the verity that emanates this place:
Refreshing, renewing, this Eden of sea and land.

The here and now is all, and all there'll be,
So here and now embrace reality.

My Beach
(or Scarlett digs for turnips)

Three days of onshore winds from the Gulf
And I walk my beach.
The beach is mine.
The beach is thine.
It's the beach of birds, of bugs, and shells,
Shells full of creatures,
Shells full of sand.
It is their beach, forevermore,
It belongs to all
And…..
The beach is mine.

Gusting winds and high, high tides
Engulf my beach,
Wash over sandbars of broken shells,
So much so
Obliterating the sand
Washed below,
My feet ankle deep
In translucent, green Gulf waters.

Ooozing soft sands
Suck my feet
Deep, deep, deep they seep.
Raising my foot to step ahead,
Reluctantly, slowly, it is released,
And a distant memory is brought to mind,
Of another place, another time.

    Of myself as a child
    Walking home from school
    In bitter cold,
    Winter's misery month
    Of snow so deep,
    Of half thawed ground,
    Winter's slushy, dirty carpet.

Stepping down from a curb
Into a unpaved street
Of mud and muck,
Sucking my feet,
Deeper and deeper
Into the mire,
Struggling, to lift my foot from the tundra
Of mud, ice, and snow.
With anger, with anguish of
Being there:
Cold, helpless creature
Sucked down into winter's cruel tar pit.

Finally…
My foot released,
Comes out of my shoe,
Out of my boot,
And losing my balance
Catching myself
With sock dangling, half-clad foot in the snow,
Anguish erupts with furious tears.
I mutter and curse,
In my childish verse.
I tell myself
"I'll not live here,"
And vow to myself
Somehow, somewhere,
To leave the North and winter's worst.

A wave comes in, splashing my legs,
Its water as warm as a bath.
It washes away that distant time,
Away that distant resentment.
The sun warms my face,
Salt air lifts my soul,
I allow myself a silent laugh,
And thankful now,
A warm little smile,
Giaconda smile of contentment.

Pas des deux

With morning's brightness, they come upon their stage:
White sands, deep green mangrove vegetation,
Intense blue of the tropic sky,
Causing all who pass them to stop in awe.

His costume: dull green shorts, soft yellow sweatshirt, and
Hat, a khaki green, looking from whence…"down under"
In his hand he holds a small bell, as he
Walks along the beach….the wide, white beach.

She is there with him, perfectly camouflaged,
Her feathers, a creamy gold accented by a few
Long, soft green tail feathers, untethered,
Secure in their daily routine, secure in ritual.

She nudges the hairs on the back of his neck
With her curved beak and head, moving freely to
Shoulder, or arm, at will: this lovely lorikeet,
With the love, the trust, the passion of her life.

high…high…high…
in the sky
they fly…no…
more…they soar…
through intense, deep blue
of this sky…
sky deeper…higher…dominating
the all of this life…

every cloud, ever known, is here…
but best, and favorite…the cirrus,
highest of the high,
form delicate wisps of white
splayed 'cross the deep blue zenith…
and once…late afternoon sun
light…refracted in a cirrus cloud
caused…
an areolar glow…of wonder…
inspiring thoughts of angelic apparitions…
of miracles…
miracles of this life…so

through this wonder…this magic…
they fly…
most often alone…
though sometimes seen
in twos or threes…
their dark, angled wings
silhouetted…
solitary…
the frigate bird…
fated to fly, to soar, through most of life
above the fray of those below…above us all…
in solitary peace…
in isolation, from this life…

Hurricane Irene

The shore is deserted
in anticipation of what comes.
Jacket clutched close around my shoulders,
I walk the beach
to clear my mind
of all that troubles.
Wild salt air
touches my lips,
its reassuring taste
not enough to dissuade
thoughts of
that which has happened,
and what may happen next.
The wind builds,
catching, carrying, grains of sand
that sting my face and eyes,
distracting concentration.

"She's coming!"
"She's coming!"
cry two harried spoonbills
as they fly overhead.
"Take care!" they cry,
rose-pink brilliance
against the dark sky.
"Take care! Take care!"
"I will," my reply.

I look up and see
the other
oncoming,
encircling,
an awesome mass
of gray and black and black and gray,
wind and force,
of course,
rises up before me saying:

"How could this happen?
How could this be?
I'm angered, I'm bothered.
I'm hot.
I'm cold.
Depression,
can't stand it!
won't have it!...
I'll cast my forces
in all directions,
destroy all
in my path.
I will have my way!

And you,
simpering
in delusional self pity,
come join me for my vengeance,
turbid havoc commences.
Throw tantrums!
Scream tirades!
Loose frustrations, and satisfy!
Clear your mind!
Cleanse your soul!"

Then shrieking out of control,
winds whistling,
howling wrath,
clouds explode
torrents of rain...
tension releasing tears...tears of rage.
I turn away
as the fury behind me unleashes.
I watch the coconut palm,
its delicate fronds lifted skyward
helplessly flailing,
buffeted by frantically
changing winds...
Are my efforts as futile?

Tears well up,
and I wonder if
my fury too, will find release.

September's Dragonflies

there…
above the jasmine they convene,
flight through, and into
faint, soft breeze…
with ease…
a low, buzzing, whirring proclivity…
to be there…

doubled, angled, shimmering, gossamer wings
to omnipresent, iridescent fuselage…
mirage…
multiplicity to be seen…
shimmer blue-gray and green…
an organized, disordered mass of
muttering, fluttering delicacy…
why there, and now, this convocation brings
this complicity of instinct
which flies and sings
rhapsodic buzz, canto keen…
why this need to be there…

then…
off on the horizon just above,
the large shape rises…
engines drone and roar,
a power, a force of
majesty…
onward it flies
commanding the skies,
large insect eyes,
rotary chopping blades whirl dramatically…
now above the fragile, odonatic cloud,
the giant spectre passes,
as a sovereign in revue,
of its retinue,
subdues the lesser, lowly, lower classes.
its passing overhead, causes sentiments of dread,
a momentary lull in the fragile little crowd,

slight dispersal of formation,
confused concentration…
a fluttering insecurity,
fleeting shroud…

but…
as the giant flies away,
their song now in contrast
soto voce as they fly…
a momentary quiver,
shaking off the frightful shiver,
of that huge,
that monstrous insect in the sky…
and once more…
rapport…
reigns…
the fluttering, insectile cloud,
continues on its way,
reaffirming once again its need,
to be there…

Jesus Freak*

green, on gray, on gray, on green,
back bay sheen, shimmer, shadow and mist,
through garua**, Monet subtleties…a wisp
of movement…or a dream
attracts…
focus is challenged,
energy of spirit
captures the eye
to identify
illusions of the miraculous…

a small gray heron,
rakishly thin,
angles and flap,
whirling, swirling,
intense in pursuit,
thrust and parry, and prance…
on surface perchance…?
ethereal predator,
intense in need,
illusions of the miraculous…

no awed disciples this to behold,
only these eyes, and
this bemused smile
to marvel this dance,
pirouette of chance…?
flickering, angled multiplicity of guile,
flurry, mist, and flap,
mirage adapt…
gavotte of illusions…and need…indeed…
illusions of the miraculous…

*Where I live, there is a tidal bay, created by a mangrove peninsula, be-
tween my balcony and the Gulf beyond. The bay is full of fish and at
low tide, birds are there fishing to feed themselves. I often see these
small gray herons, "Reddy Herons," fishing and am reminded of the
biblical story of Jesus walking on water, as these birds appear to be

walking on water. In my mind I call these birds "Jesus Freaks" no disrespect, no insult intended.

**garua: a South American word meaning more than mist and less than a drizzle.

The Stork and the Crone

At water's edge, long-legged stands,
Subservient to instinct's strict commands,
Here in the warmth of morning's sun
An old woodstork from northern lands.

Unconcerned with passersby,
So relieved now not to fly,
Wondering, was this flight his last,
Weary, life does mystify.

She watches him with clouded eye,
Floaters mar the sunlit sky,
And pondering her own fragility,
Meets his eye to verify

The morning's truth, she breathes a sigh,
All pretense now gone awry,
The stork in gentle sympathy,
Blinks and winks his knowing eye.

Diva

(the great white egret in the spring mating season)

> She promenades for all to view,
> Her swaying skirts, white lace filigree.
> Her gaze down her long face says to you,
> "You may covet, desire, and worship me."
>
> Around her eyes a bright iridescence:
> Cool contrast, a viridian green.
> Elegance, regality, pervade her essence,
> She is at once both a seductress, and a queen.
>
> Feathery, white fringes softly frame
> Her lovely head, with disarming grace.
> Elegant, long black-stockinged legs,
> Slowly step with deliberate pace.
>
> Reviewing her subjects 'round the pond,
> She's a blend of seduction and disdain.
> Hers is a fascination Cleopatra could have spun…
> It is the season for her reign.

(Yes, I know it was probably a male egret that I saw displaying himself in the mating season, but this, the pretense of a female egret, makes a more entertaining image.)

Unpredicted, Unexpected

The storm of the century had not occurred,
But local predictions were right on target,
Cool winds from the north, twenty-plus miles per hour,
Setting a scene not to forget:

A shining morning, crisp, sunlit, and dancing,
And there above the vast white beach,
A "Blue Angel" performance, enthralling, entrancing,
Ability, agility, beyond man's reach.

Two ospreys, expressing their joy of being,
Fly loop-the-loops, circles, breathtaking dives,
Aerial feats, one never dreamt of seeing,
Figure eight series, flight alive.

Their wings swept back, tiny fighter jets,
No time to question their reasons why,
As they catch these winds on this glorious set,
What sheer delight it must be to fly!

The Pelican

Splashing in at a low angle,…(the lagoon
is so shallow)…folds its seven-foot
wingspan, waggles its tail feathers, and bobbing its
body-long beak up and down, swallows a

wriggling, cold wet, scaly fish,
then glides on the lagoon's surface,
despite ungainly, awkward appearance,
with the grace of a swan.

Wings lifted high, a few flaps carry it into the air.
Slight body movements navigate
its course, soaring over the
horizontal surface.

With uncanny casualness, in mid-flight it
reaches 'round with its beak to nibble
an itch on its foot:
four pounds of unglamorous, unpretentious….cool!

Grace Note

Trying its best to be all things to all,
A mockingbird boldly is perched on a wall,
Warbling and chirping
A myriad of songs,
Indiscriminate babble,
Musical rabble,
Mimicking every call ever heard,
Absurd,
Wayward, misguided, ridiculous bird.

In the cyberspace speed of life,
In the hurry and expedience,
Necessity's lack of tolerance,
In the hope to impress, race for success…
Are finesse, and understatement lost?
In irrational grasping
At indiscriminate straws…
Sidestepping of laws…
Is the joy of uniqueness…ignored…the cost?

The grace note, delicately played and refined,
Softened staccato, enhancing the line,
Artful reticence…
Disciplined technique cascade.
Is consciousness entered, the delicacy known…or
Does the rondo swoosh…and
Dissolve past the ear,
Not to hear,
Disappear, as though never played?

The nutty flavor of Darjeeling tea,
Leaves gathered from trees
On a certain hill, at a certain time,
In a certain province…of
India.
Is the subtlety noted?…savored?…or
Is the brewing, and effort…
A futility?…
Lost in distraction's mutability…?

The red-winged blackbird's unique song,
Its trill, a delicate flourish,
Creates a mystique, a
Magic, and transcendence…
Shimmering…
As the iridescence
Of the many hued sheen
On fluttering black wings…
A grace to be noted, and cherished.

Morning Walk

They walk down the beach,
An older couple,
Unique only in their lack of need for trying.
No pomp of stature,
No style of dress,
Unpretentious,
No swagger, gesture, or determined physical strife,
No drama of the obvious,
No "Look a' me!" attitude.

Their quiet conversation with one another,
Speaks to all who would see,
Of long life together, their dream still unfolding...enfolding...
Clasped hands,
Fingers, entwined like their lives,
Swing gently back and forth
With the sway, the rhythm of their stroll,
And the soft breeze of May's morning.

Tears well up in these eyes
At the realization of the beauty in the moment just passed.

I look out to the sea at first light,
    Misty blue, muted gray,
    In the dawn of the day,
The sea is still filled with the night.

Then, the sky fills with clouds, and by them kissed,
    Overcast, light suffused,
    Shadowed sea is bemused,
Saturated with fog, and with mist.

But in the clear of the bright afternoon,
    Rich blue-green, so intense,
    Unlimited, immense,
On and on, the sea dances its tune.

At sunset, sea and sky in array,
    And the glory now fuller,
    In a riot of color,
Celebrating the joy of the day.

In the night, I look out to afar,
    The sea, black and darkling,
    Surface bright, shining, sparkling,
Reflecting the moon and the stars.

The Hurricane Season

The tree was broken in two,
Bottom, still verdant, strong, and flourishing,
But completely dismembered upon the ground,
Twisted top, shattered, withered and brown,
September's storms taking their due.
Rainy season, lush and nourishing,
Can bring winds of wrath, beating all in their path,
All victims of hurricane season.

I remember the spring of life, half seeing, half knowing,
Ignoring the spectre of consequence.
Learning the ways to live in the times,
With youthful, strong self-confidence.
Taking on with agility, with naive gullibility,
Knowing not what to do, without faintest clue,
Ignorant of life's fragility,
Oblivious to hurricane season.

But now, in frustrated anxiety,
Uncertain of propriety,
Confusion, misdirection, complacent disorder,
Cause an overload to reason.
Deluged by hypocrisy, drowning in mediocrity,
I too shall be broken in two.
Lost is constancy, lost hope of order,
For now is my hurricane season.

So, as harsh winds blow, fierce rains flow,
Sapping the strength of one's soul,
Utter a shudder, sigh a frisson,
It is the hurricane season.

Fledgling

It is there he has landed, beneath a parked car.
Astounded excitement, having just flown this far.
He blinks, and he thinks, of the progress he's made,
First flight on his own, landing there in the shade.
He wonders, and ponders, at life all around,
And why has he found himself, here on the ground,
And the question arises, the why and the how,
    "Now that I'm here, what do I do now?"

I think of myself, as I watch this young life,
Of all opportunities, all unknown strife
That need be dealt with, as life goes on
To reach what's next, what lies beyond.
Having reached age, with so much in the past,
From conquest, and defeat, comes the question at last,
At the end of adventure, hope will allow,
    "Now that I've gotten here,…what do I do now?"

Though years have demanded the payment of cost,
Perhaps, though experienced,…innocence is not lost.
And like this young bird with uninitiated view,
We all, need with courage, our quest to pursue.
For we all, are fledglings, in one way or another,
No matter abilities, or lack of bother.
We all, at some moment must ask somehow,
    "Now that we've gotten here, what do we do now?"

At Last...April

Jasmine blooms, fragrance on the air,
Morning's sunlight, warm and fair,
Gentle breezes, lifting care,
And the red-winged blackbird sings.

Horizon's view, white crystal sands,
Indolent care for the day's demands,
Gentle touch of loving hands,
And the red-winged blackbird sings.

Spring's morning, hushed and still,
Mesmerized by this magic trill,
Breath caught, senses thrill,
As the red-winged blackbird sings.

Blue

The great white egret,
Impossible to forget,
Its glorious luminescent white
A simple case of dander,
From feather follicles…
Molecules, of which, cause splendor
Of an elegance shining bright,
Flying in morning sunlight.
What vision could be grander?
But, as it flies into the shade,
Transition shapes the view,
Discernment can be made,
The egret has changed its hue,
It flies in shades of blue…

Once the sun shown brightly,
Serendipity lured so spritely,
All things possible to do.
But time's shadow fell across,
Innocent joy of life was lost,
And hope by cynicism knocked askew.
Grand luminescence,
Dispersed by youthful effervescence,
Caused acceptance of…
That, which is true.
So with wary, vigilant facade,
Play the grand charade,
For there's nothing left to do
But to fly…in shades of blue.

Indefatigable

In dawn's light,
Amid stones and cinders of the parking lot,
It raises itself for the coming day.
Minute drops of the night's cool mist
Have formed on its spindly, fragile leaves and stems:
Dew,
Perhaps the day's only moisture.

No matter,
With courage and determination,
It lifts its tiny head to face the day,
And slowly, each petal of the bud
Unfolds, revealing
A small, roseate, corolla bloom, mimicking
The sun's glory.

Sweet salt air surrounds,
Bathes this tiny plant, this weed,
Unexpected, unwanted,
Yet there, defying herbicides, and
Pesticides, and homicides,
And any other cides,
Man or nature can concoct.

There in the vast parking lot,
Cars coming and going, feet trampling,
Awaiting the guillotine blade of the gardener's spade,
Unnoticed,
This defiant, determined, innocence,
If only for a moment,
Prevails in beauty.

And in ages to come,
When the parking lot's gone, as gone all shall be,
With dawn,
Beauty, no matter how small, or insignificant,
Will raise itself,
Mimic morning's radiance,
And persevere.

thoughts and observations

Menov's Grace*

Expectations fell short
The efforts for those moments were his best,
Yet, lacking somehow, in some way…in what?
Strength?…no. Ability?…
Or that magic thrill of creative sensibility?
A dream that comes alive before our eyes?…
Heroically, an effort that's invincible?
Perfection, more than man can realize?
And all the while the world out there is watching.

Serenely, he accepts what fate has given.
He gives no sign of loss, for our detection,
No regret in the legacy that now is passing
Onto the next who will inspire perfection.
And with a greater grace, a choice is made,
Inherently, nobility is staid.
And as we watch the drama now unfold,
In dignity, bronze embraces gold.
And all the while the world out there, is watching.

*This took place in the year 2000 Olympic Games, Men's Gymnastics, the Russian Team. Menov, having been a star, performed less than expectations—his own and the world's. He only received the bronze award.

The Celebrity

She precedes him by a few minutes,
Statuesque, beautiful.
She selects a few things, pretty things,
Adornments for her beauty.

He enters, minutes before closing,
The shop empty, but for these two.
It is his eyes that identify him,
That look that thrilled millions,
Superstar,
Fifty years before.

His face looks like paper,
Brown paper crumpled thousands of times,
Smoothed out only to be crumpled again and again.
His hair now dyed brown,
Not the deep almost black it once was.
His stature...not as tall as expected.
Not the magnificence of the giant screen.
The phrase comes to mind:
..."Come with me to my fahdder's palace"...
A prince of the Middle East
Flawed by a Brooklyn/Jersey accent?
A major gaff in an early film.

Demurely, she asks for her few selections,
And he agrees,
Anticipating the gifts she will bring to the night.

Warily, he surveys his surroundings,
His eyes searching for response.
Aggressive arrogance there, defying recognition,
The condescending, polite niceties that must be endured.
And yet...more is there in his guarded eyes.
Behind it all,
Behind celebrity,
Behind arrogance,
Is a glint of fear...a desperate glint of terror...
Terror...of not being
Recognized.

Good Grief!

Standing second in a line of two,
I wait my turn.

"I'll handle this," one clerk says,
"You take care of the next."

"Oh, that's okay," says the second clerk,
"There's nobody else here."

Nobody else here?
What am I then
Sprinkled with the questionable dust
Of invisible anonymity?

True, I stand here with no artifice
To appearance, face or hair,
But quake at the injustice
Oblivious ignorance,
Unconcerned with granting dignity
To another's plain banality?
Are we so mesmerized by gilded lilies
That we no longer acknowledge reality?

"Good Grief!"
"I'm here!"

The Carousel Ride

The wheelchair approaches the carousel ride,
    An atrophied body so small,
A boy? No a man, the mustache belies,
    Twisted shape causes me to appall.

Having pushed him this far, a token she buys,
    She lifts him to go on the ride.
The loveseat for them is just the right size,
    On her lap snuggled close to her side.

And around they go, and around some more,
    She croons and she talks in his ear,
And he gently nestles, as he's done before,
    And it certainly does appear,

He's an infant, a coddling, her dear, sweet babe,
    In spite of the long endless time
She's carried and cared for this life to save,
    No time for herself to pine.

In my mind I question what courage is this,
    What selfless and determined love?
As the ride ends she lifts him and gives him a kiss,
    Her burden, her gift from above.

Steadfastly she lowers him back in his chair,
    For she has conquered her fears.
She smiles as she fondly tousles his hair,
    And it is I who is left in tears.

Artificial Flowers

They're held by many in outright affection,
An esteem to question, and try to discover
A relevance worthy of circumspection,
Their attraction an enigma to uncover.
They reign in faded dust covered perfection,
In homes, showrooms, offices, and municipal towers:
Plastic shapes, plastic colors, displayed with much bother.
I never cared much for artificial flowers.

Real flowers are those that defy perfection,
Irregular color, shape like no other.
Their fragile beauty defies deception,
While watching they fade, and their lives are rather
An illusion, a fragment, a dream recollection,
Of peace and beauty in fragrant bowers.
Reality, their fragrance could almost smother.
I never cared much for artificial flowers.

People too, may have on further reflection,
A callous shell, a facade, a cover,
A plastic soul, that on inspection,
Insight and instinct soon discover
An artifice, shallow, easily found detection
Of lies, deceptions, and crass bids for power
By officials, friends, and yes, even lovers......
I never cared much for artificial flowers.

So could the games be played, one to another
Without need for pretense, without need to cower,
But open and caring, and truth rediscover?
Perhaps not, the way of the world overpowers.
But...I never cared much for artificial flowers.

Irises

The ranting soul in the public place,
Naked, injured nerve endings,
Throbbing in public disgrace.
"Why hast thou forsaken me?"
Terror in tirade....
We turn away embarrassed faces,
Blushing giggles hide confusion,
Some even run away,
Chaos in profusion.
What decision, what action next?
The rules have all been broken.
"Play nice!" the teacher had said.

In front of a shop, a bundle of rags,
Sleeping bones, and skin, and dirt,...a hag.
And why is she there,
What brought her to be
This wretch, this lost humanity?
And why am I here, why am I me?
And why is it I am not lost as she?

Caressingly, I stroke the cat.
But it in turn, turns and clamps its teeth
Around my thumb.
It hesitates, as I, in good faith, wait.
But then it surely tightens its jaws,
Breaking the skin,
And blood spills into my palm.
Pain is my lesson.
The book explains it as dominance:
Preferring control, to the caress.

And where is God in all of this?
    All-knowing father in the sky?
    Particles of atoms hurtling by?
    Decisions made by you or I?
And what sensitivity did we miss?

What decision did the ranting soul make? What direction, the
hag in rags forsake? What actions about them did we take?
　　　Bite? or purr?
　　Or is it all just a search for bliss?

When the sun warms the earth,
The strong shoots emerge,
Strengthen in time, 'til bud and bloom appear,
And glorious
The color, grace, and radiance, for a few days.
But time, wind, and rain, dominate the blooms,
And they wither, and fold in on themselves,
'Til plucked and thrown to earth,
And by minute creatures, rent to pieces…humus…
Ashes to ashes,
Dust to dust,
The sun also rises…and we…
We are debris.

Kirttimukha*

The cat's teeth bit into my hand,
Canines deeply puncturing.
Scratches too,
Clawing away shreds of skin,
Instantaneous pain,
Startled reflex responses.

    She was frightened,
    My hand, the closest thing to attack,
    Defending herself against constant inevitability.

As healing occurs in my hand,
In my mind, thoughts of why?
Why such pain?
Why such fear, such panic in her, to
Inflict, to cause such pain?

    Why indeed, a benevolent, loving,
    Forgiving God
    Includes these into the intricate designs of life?

I watch the constant wariness,
Never-ending vigilance for survival,
The absence of trust in wild things,
The brutality of instant, merciless attack,
Predators bringing down their prey,
The violent feeding frenzy,
Being eaten alive by another creature
Before death's mercy.

    A child missing in Colorado,
    The only thing found…
    Tracks of a mountain lion on his trail…
    Imagine the child's horror…
    Is this God's divine plan?…
    Fear, unendurable pain, and horror?

The Hindus have a legend of Kirttimukha:
"Face of Glory"
The monstrous face of that, that is life…
A being that eats itself to survive.

> Recognizing the nature of life,
> (Not just idealized wishes or assumptions)
> And accepting its sometimes brutality,
> Its sometimes inevitability,
> Is difficult…
> The human heart and understanding,
> Searches for the ideal,
> But sometimes finds the unbearable.
> Accepting both…is life's reality.

*"Myths to Live By"
By Joseph Campbell
"The Confrontation of East and West in Religion"

Voyeur, Voyeuse

You go to see a film that is "R"-rated.
Your own life has been something of a botch.
And though the plot is weak and overstated,
You're hoping to see a scene or two of crotch.
    And so voyeur, voyeuse,
    Producers hire Tom Cruise:
They're banking on how much you like to watch.

In speech you use not words, but acronyms,
Easy cliché, and rude vulgarity.
You overlook your lazy language sins,
Your speech approaching, therefore, incongruity.
    And so voyeur, voyeuse,
    Apply your self abuse,
Whole thought expressed by you is such a rarity.

Let no one in, don't try your life at living.
Stay in your space, and safely bar the door.
Spurn chance, and sweet romance so unforgiving,
Though solitary life can be a bore.
    And so voyeur, voyeuse,
    Your life becomes obtuse.
Perhaps you'd like a little something more.

Life, and love, and passion, and compassion,
Are all too complicated and demanding.
Failure and rejection of your fashion,
Threaten self containment of your standing.
    And so voyeur, voyeuse,
    Your grace, is in disuse,
Isolation answers to your life's commanding.

But TV fills your need in just a moment,
With talking heads, soap operas, you're relaxed.
And life may be purchased for only three installments,
On your credit card, if not already maxed.
    And so voyeur, voyeuse,
    You now will be seduced,
And never will your energies be taxed!

So life, homogenized and sugar-coated,
With pre-digested thought and inquiry,
Fills your mind until it has truly over bloated
Your complacent self and sated reverie.
    And so voyeur, voyeuse,
    Your self worth you reduce,
You've stroked your so inflated vanity.

Your voyeuristic watching is lascivious,
With self gratifying senses, like a civet.
Thus, you go through life, somewhat oblivious
To the cunning vagaries of those who give it.
    And so voyeur, voyeuse,
    This is the way you choose,
It's easier to watch life…than to live it.

Yougottas

Yougotta do this!
Yougotta do that!
    And to inure
    Your mien insure,
Yougotta feed the cat!

Yougotta wake up early,
And if you're feeling surly,
    You must prepare
    With special care
Your countenance as pearly.

Yougotta think "so."
Yougotta make "dough."
    But don't decline
    To "fall in line,"
Or down and down you'll go.

Yougotta acquiesce
To power's faux finesse.
    For if you don't,
    Or if you won't.
Your life will be a mess.

Yougotta buy the hype
Of propaganda's tripe,
    For not to do
    Will label you
An antisocial snipe.

Yougotta get the jump
On some less witted chump.
    Yougotta do,
    You must pursue,
Or else you're in the dump!

Yougotta do it now.
Yougotta act with pow!
    You must produce,
    Status induce,
And who's to care just how?

Yougotta make the deal.
Yougotta deal with zeal.
    Yougotta sell
    Yourself as well,
If necessary steal.

Yougotta tell a lie.
Yougotta answer why.
    And don't presume
    A truth may loom,
    And soon regret
    Will find you yet,
    And all is lost
    Yourself the cost,
    And hope is naught
    For honor's caught.
Yougotta do or die.

Yougotta tell the truth.
Yougotta make it "smooth."
    Noblesse oblige
    Assume with ease.
Yougotta tell, forsooth!

Yougotta do alot.
Yougotta do......or not!
    And in the end,
    Your choice my friend!
Life's battle gamely fought!

Morning Faces,
the 8:30 AM ferry commute—20 minutes

Dazed, darting, blotchy, red, bleary eyes,
search with predatory mania
for that cup of comfort with the surge to jump start reality….
caffeine.

Busily chatty matrons, on their way to shop
with too quickly, too brightly made up faces
that do not hide the tired manacles of
too early a start,
slept on coifs at angles and straggles,
yet attempting bright exuberance and outwitting.

The tradesman's lined, weathered face,
though quiet,
eyes click like computers
weighing commitments against probabilities,
belying outward calm,
his day already well under way.

The young…children and teens,
unaware of the glow of life and radiance
from fresh, rosy, creamy cheeks and lips,
oblivious to the wonder of life that they are,
are intent on their tunnel visions of their yet unexplored selves.

The morning jogger,
with introspected mania of self control and superiority,
too restless to sit,
stretches, and emanates self-willed health.

The face of the professional woman,
with well-groomed, well-tailored confidence,
is closed, as she opens her briefcase to get
a novel in which she loses herself for a few moments,
escaping her well ordered life
if only for a short time.

The older gentleman reading his newspaper,
ivoried face…hair silvered, and elegant,
as are his dated clothes,
dismisses, and overlooks the confusion and bustle around him,
willing the sedateness of his life.

The college student on the way to classes,
clean-faced and unpretentious,
intently in a book,
cramming, making use of each minute of the day's busy schedule.

The crew's faces
healthy with the nature of their world and the sea air,
wrapped up in uniforms and routines,
and well placed smiles and niceties.

The ferry arrives.
We dock and go our separate ways,
changing our faces as the day progresses,
and as challenges are met or avoided,
or that cup of comfort is found.

Snapshot

"Mother, do you remember?"
Expectantly, she hands me the snapshot: A young woman
Lifting a laughing child
High out of the waters of a swimming pool.

Searching recall brings nothing but
The dull blow of realization:
I don't remember,
Not time, not place,
Not pool, not face,
That could not have been me.
Yet...
The brows are right...the hairline too,
And the crooked tooth,
Yes, that could have been mine,
But memory even abandons the child
In excited gaiety of splash:
To have forgotten my own child
Now thirty some years later before me?

"Well?" she asks.

"I don't remember
Having been that pretty
Or that happy...."
And the melancholia of forgotten times and forgotten places
envelops.

Alchemy

A slight disorientation,
Imbalance,
A loss…of what?
Assurance that all is well?
Is all…not well?
Why this sense of frantic ennui?
What's denied the cerebrum
To alter equilibrium?

If only to talk to.
No…she's not there:
Idea backboard,
Reality compunction
To relieve dysfunction.
She's gone away,
A short, short stay,
To that city of fertile, alluvial plains.

If just to call,
But where?
And why?…there is no need,
She'll be back soon.
It's not the calling,
It's knowing I could,
Her happy voice,
My lucky touchstone,
Assures life's rationality.

Tango

Primeval, throbbing pulse,
Pulsating, murky fantasy,
Exquisite, melodic siren
    beckoning hidden, suppressed darknesses
Of unrequired, unrequited, frustrated passions
    smoldering, moldering,
in a yet unknown place.

A cry, a soliloquy,
An appealing lament for emotion never expressed.
Joy and rapture only hoped for,
    never realized…
    broken promise of life.

Yet, the throbbing beat goes on,
    inviting…inciting.
    an ephemeral hope,
Opening dark places of regret,
    and yet…

Stroking, and stroking the soul,
The haunting, rhapsodic lament offers
    a perversion of joy…
    of dreams never realized.

Décor

Rooms are filled with so many views to ponder,
Scenes that drive serenity deep asunder,
Like a gang of hooligans come to plunder,
Trashed like a gutter.

Frills, and foils, and swags, and swatches,
Faux finesse, a mismatch of hues and blotches,
Figurines, a gargoyle with eyes who watches
Me as I shudder.

Disarray of photographs for beholding,
Dusty knick knacks, forgotten keys, unfolding
Papers, books, a cup with a teabag molding,
Enough, I mutter.

Give me simple elegance unencumbered.
Do away with frivolous lines unnumbered.
Outlook fresh, clairvoyance now plain and humbler.
Spare me the clutter.

Toulouse: the Seventy Pound, Pit Bull, Lapdog

The seventy pound, pit bull, lapdog,
    Is sleeping now next to my knee.
The rumbling sound of a fat frog,
    His snoring just fills me with glee!

On the end of my sofa he's sleeping,
    Sublime in his tenacity,
My vigilant care he is keeping,
    His duty is to protect me.

Awake his brown eyes show a deepness,
    Faithful and true clarity,
Brave intelligent deep velvet sweetness,
    Bestowing his sincerity.

But I ask myself why, with his great size,
    And his large web-footed feet,
His delusions of Chihuahua guise?
    He must think himself somewhat petite!

So on my lap there's a round, brutish, fat log,
    Oblivious to his great size,
The seventy pound, pit bull, lapdog,
    The dearest of friends in my eyes

Perplexity

Confusion revolves through my cranium,
As I contemplate each new geranium,
    Each hue I behold,
    From crimson to gold,
Is really too much for my brainium!

So perhaps I should choose white titanium,
Or salmon might be more germainium,
    But despite what I choose,
    My wits I do lose,
For you see, I love all quite the sameium!

The Word...or the poet's dilemma

Quite, trite, in the middle of the night,
Up, tight, a word I need to write.
First, light, no answers are in sight.
I need to find a word to rhyme,
A word that is just right.

Mid, day, my mind is still at play.
Thoughts, stray, confusion rules the day.
Gang, way, a thought has come my way:
A word I've heard, I've found a word,
That's precisely what to say.

"Your hair looks pretty today."

I look up from work as he passes by.
I had given no sign, no furtive eye.
Had not even known that he was there
Until his compliment on my hair.

"Your hair looks pretty today."
What a lovely thing to say.

I did not know him, never saw him before.
And most likely I would see him nevermore.
I wonder what prompted his gentle care,
To tell me he liked my silvered hair.

Women compliment me all the time on style,
But men never, never, in such a long while.
As a girl I remember the boys with soft sighs,
Would follow my golden hair with their eyes.

But years have turned the gold to ash,
And compliments from men are all in the past.
And now "nevermore," I greet with a sigh
My turn being over, I whisper goodbye

To the honor that men used to lavish on me.
Until unexpected I look up and see,
A silver haired prince serendipity's sent,
To offer a long awaited compliment:

"Your hair looks pretty today."
What a sweet, lovely thing to say.

A Shakespearean Sampler for a Young Girl

Yon handsome Romeo has a lean and hungry look,
But lovely Juliet, do have a care.
Don't build your dreams on something from a storybook.
Don't fool yourself expecting what's not there.

Every prince, no matter how sweet and charming,
Has his own aggressions and ambitions.
So no matter his attentions so disarming,
Remember your small portion of his intentions.

If with my intrusion I've offended,
With such a dreary metaphor, I know,
Think but this, my dear, and all is mended,
Life is what you'd settle for, and so

    Unto thine own self be true, be blithe and bonny.
    Cry no more and sing, "Hey, nonny, nonny!"

They've Planned Their Own Reunion

I was the last one told,
But who am I to scold?
Nuance leads me to understand
My offsprings' silent reprimand:
    "Mother, we're grown."
    "We're on our own."
    "Leave us alone."

If I can't say anything,
I won't say anything at all.
The whir of the beaters whipping
The frothy satisfaction
Of my "Blackberry Cloud Pie."
    I lick the spoon.
    It's almost noon.
    They'll be here soon.

A Would-Be Perfect Life

What would I think the perfect life to be?
    More hours in the day, and the energy to do
All the things that I choose, and the places to see,
    And sleep every night more that ten hours, too
    And rife opportunities to smell all the flowers.
    Perhaps a new planet with thirty-six hours.

From the sill I select a most perfect nectarine,
    Its form and color are beyond belief.
But tasting its flesh, thoughts and senses careen:
    No sweetness, no flavor, no acidic relief.
    So is this what we search for in every direction:
    Tasteless and joyless, deceptive perfection?

Within us we carry the wonder we seek,
    No matter our searching wherever we go.
And like poor Pierrot, with his sad tearful cheeks,
    We can't see perfection on the end of our nose.
    These elusive answers are really that simple.
    This great truth, however, may just be a pimple.

Romance

Raised…eyes…meet…
    and suddenly hearts skip a beat,
Coyly…enjoying…
    another sideward glance or two.
Thoughts…so…sweet…
    excitement builds, reason retreats.
Falling so in love is just an act of
    one's imagination.

Preparing for the recital

I escaped winter this year
fleeing to my beloved peninsula.
But come May, I find myself
in my daughter's home, which is

embedded in the angled side
of a sheltering Rocky Mountain.
I gaze through the dining room window.
After all avoidance, I watch

the silent, silent snow fall straight down on
protruding rock adorned
in a white lace mantle
of peace and solitude.

Three young bull elk,
their antlers winter shorn to mere nubbins,
in the spring twilight silently follow one another
Indian style across the scene.

Erin's small hands begin to practice
"Ode to Joy" on the cherrywood piano
in the living room. The sky darkens, and the elk
disappear in the dusky curtain of snow.

Skeet

The racing cycle takes the curve,
An image spare and lean,
Meshed gears whirr
With skill and verve,
A finely tuned machine.
    Senses surrender.

So long ago I was the coach.
My efforts were for naught,
For when it came to basketball,
I was the one being taught.
Despite my fine routine,
    Little help could I render...

Everyone called her Skeet,
Totally lacking attitude,
Modest, calm, and bright,
The thing of most significance
Was the way she moved...
Smooth...efficient...
Like a finely-tuned machine.
Understated grace and elegance,
A silent whirr of radiance,
    Her eloquent agenda.

In time I've seen others,
Michael Jordan and Grant Hill,
Who delivered with quiet confidence
The required grace and skill.
But for finely-tuned responses, still,
    Hers is the name I remember.

    She must be in her sixties...
    Then...I wonder what her life has been.

The Ballad of Sneaky Pete's

The drummer sets the beat of the grove,
Guitars and keyboard, efforts pool,
Searching for the nirvana of "cool,"
And those understanding, can't help but move.

Enter young "wanna-be's," just slightly damaged,
Only tinged by disillusion,
Hep to this profusion,
Presenting a "cool" well managed.

The old "would-have-been," gone to pot,
Remembering with tried hearts and minds,
Celebrate justly with their own kinds,
An illusion of "cool" not forgot.

And here we all are, at Sneaky Pete's.

Others, seated at the bar with drink,
Dissolving their pains with a boozy smile,
Seeking oblivion, if just for a while,
A while of not having to think.

Beyond the bar, ignoring the scene,
Hustlers, real and would-be "cool,"
Quest for triumph in a game of pool,
Covet the pride of winning the green.

Determined waitresses, to satisfy want,
Hustle food, and drink, and celebration,
With smiles, and guiles, and anticipation,
They joke and charm in bon vivant.

Watching the action at Sneaky Pete's

The "would-be-elite," slumming to impress,
Take a few moments to ease their souls,
Ease preconceived coveted roles,
Finding release from perceived distress.

The "bleary-eyed-has-been," stumbling around,
Searching for a "used-to-be-sweet-young-thing,"
A memory of what it once had been
To be the "hero-found."

On the dance floor, "gyrating-memories,"
Of having been a "flower-child,"
Of having once been young and wild,
Momentarily lost in reveries.

    Dealing and dancing at Sneaky Pete's.

Parents, grandparents, watch and smile
At feet bouncing, curls tossing, to the beat of the band,
A piece of pizza held in her hand,
The dance of a beloved child.

The "uncommitted" observing profusion,
Missing the point
Of this joyful joint,
Bemused by this organized confusion.

With all this observance, there comes a sigh,
For the ordered efforts to abandon fears,
To nullify stress with laughter and tears,
And the question evolves: "Why am I?"

    "Hooray! I say, for Sneaky Pete's!"

Reflection

Mid-morning,
Sky, clear, bright blue,
And clouds, a few,
Fluffy cumulus, white and cheerful.
But that to the south?
A small weak cloud? A veil of mist?
No.
At the end of her cycle,
A faint, fading wisp:
The moon, waning in her last quarter.

Not the new, hopeful crescent
Smiling in the evening sky.
Nor the radiant, lush full beauty
Gracing night's darkness.
Just the remnants of that wonder,
Lost in the bright bustle of morning's ambitions.
A ghost of herself, barely seen.
A nuage of what she once had been.
And in this, the end of her cycle,
I see myself, and what I have become:
The frail, pale shadow, of that which I once was.

Hyacinth

In pre-dawn darkness,
Familiarities obscured,
Its newly acquired presence on the windowsill
Revealed only by fragrance fresh and delicate.
My barely awakened senses
Fumbling with routine, regimen, necessities,
Brought up short by this fresh preview,
The promise of spring to come
Vaguely, your words drift back into my consciousness:

    "We'll plant the bulbs here
    along the walkway,
    and then next spring
    they will sprout, blossom,
    be fragrant and beautiful."

Memory of your "pre-dawn" regimen:
You would sit at the kitchen table in the dark
With black coffee and cigarettes, silent and alone.
And now all these years later,
Darkly solitaire for a few moments before day begins,
Stretching, and breathing in dawn's sweet air,
An epiphany of understanding occurs:
Soul's desperate need for a few undemanded upon moments alone
To protect self…and sanity.

    The lessons you taught so long ago,
    Behaviors…examples set…
    Plant the seed, or notion,
    And it will grow into something beautiful,
    Be it flower, or love, or the integrity of one's soul.

Circle of Kindness

In consonance we meet,
Moments shared together,
Ideas, emotions too discreet,
We open, to glimpse a view,
Of what we hope is true…whatever…
And you…my fellows, my friends…listen
As my heart and mind I pour
Into your kind reception,
For, few moments,…nothing more.

Those closest to our emotion,
Love us not for what is real,
But for how we make "them" feel.
Their distraction fails to listen,
Self absorption fails to hear,
What is near,…what is dear?
Polite boredom their reaction.

So we give, and give some more…hoping for…
A birth…
An epiphany of ourselves…
(How in turn they make us feel.)
But, expectations must be met, rituals kept…
Not ourselves, but goals they've set
The criteria of our worth…so…

These hoarded thoughts,
Secreted away in my mind's eye…I
Unveil to you, for moments few.
Your grace allows me freedom…
Ideas, frustrations flow,
And perhaps a thought takes hold…or twists…
To cause a tear, or smile…beguile…
Perhaps…? perhaps…?

For your thoughtful mental caress, attentive tenderness,
Compassionate dear friends,
I thank you.

Golden Halcyon*

There was a day in fall so amber bright,
With fingers splayed, King Midas swept the skies,
Thus turning all to golden rays of light,
And just to see it made my spirits rise.

My camera forgotten, my chagrin
At being unprepared this light to capture.
And yet, in truth, mere film could not begin
To catch this glowing air in joyous rapture.

It would require a Monet or Van Gogh
To seize the haloed light that graced this day.
But though that day is gone, I surely know
I've something of this wonder that will stay:

Its memory's kept where joy can't go awry,
It safely dwells within my own mind's eye.

*This occurred one beautiful fall day, at a cottage south of Lexington, Michigan, on Lake Huron.

Conversations with Migratory Geese

By my morning window
Drinking tea,
Caffeine to start my energies,
Organize my thought, I

First hear a pre-emptive squawk,
Then another, then bursting
Into the sunlit sky above,
I see them come,
Honking their celebratory conversations,
A raucous, cacophony of joy and purpose,
In perfect V-form flying
Straight into my view…above…
And over…

Thoughts go back forty years
To an afternoon
Incapacitated with the nausea
Of morning sickness.
Through misery, I heard
Their joyous honking above,
Their migratory return from winter
Bringing hope
And the promise of new life.

That was spring.
Now it is fall.
Time for preparation to leave.

How many grains of sand remain, I wonder?
Make them joyous, their reply.

The Loner Savant

Left alone, by parents: preoccupied.
Left alone, by peers as odd.
Left alone, by husband: for others more charming.
Left alone, by children: gone to grown lives.
Left alone, with loneliness: the loneliness of years.
Left alone, 'til the penance becomes blessing.
And she who emerges
Is the loner savant,
Wise in the ways of solitude,
Whose soul's sanity silently screams
Leave me alone.
Leave me…alone.
Leave me…
Alone.

She Dances

She dances in tiny silver tap shoes,
Fifty on one side,
Fifty on the other,
Changing from one tiny complicated step
To another, legs and feet
Trying to keep up with the nuance
Of ever changing tempos,
Her long body follows, as a conga line.

She dances on sheer Zildjian brass,
Multi-mixed vibrations
Blend to a soft, lustrous whirr,
While a chorus of tiny silver crickets sing
An ode to stress and hysteria,
As I wrangle with the jangle of the mangle in my mind…
She dances.

Melancholy

Breathe in…
Breathe…out…and…
    Sigh…vaguely wondering why…
    Thoughts…float…around…
Like a dream…
    nothing's quite as it
Seems…wondering though…
Could it be so?…or…is…
All…of it a lie, that you
    tell yourself?
    What has happened…
And now…what to do.
    as time slips away?…

    All…should…be…
Wonderfully bright…
Like the glow of a soft summer's night…
    Why…then…this…haunt…
    this vague malaise…
That invades and delays…so…
    Why…so…resigned to this?
    Search…through…your…mind…
And search the soul…of…
    your dream's…sad…dark…pall…
    So now…so wrong…
Hear…the small tear…
    gently…fall…

Full Circle

The large album opened like a book: six pockets holding
Six fragile records, black, shiny grooves, 78 rpms.
Each side, one song in length, twelve songs in the album.
Labels as yet indiscernible, but the recordings…
Treated as rare treasures.

The record player, a large rectangular box,
Covered with tweedy fabric, tans, and blacks in color.
The needle, in the arm that read the vibrations,
Was frequently checked and changed,
Held in place by a small thumb screw.

When turned on, and a record played,
An inconceivable magic occurred:
The guitar, brilliant, the violin, a passion unknown before.
Two gypsy souls, awakening first concepts of music:
Thirties style swing jazz, from "The Hot Club of Paris."

Sixty-some years pass.
78s are collector's items.
45s, LPs, and cassettes are passé.
Analog recording is old fashioned, and
Digital rules…so

After Brubeck and Shearing,
After the Beatles, Fleetwood Mac, and the Stones,
After the French Impressionists, DeBussy, Ravel,
After the brilliance of Chopin, the eloquence of Mozart,
And Bach's supreme rightness,

The small, black-buttoned CD player plays
Twenty-four songs, the whole album on one small 4 3/4" disc.
Once more, the music of the two gypsies is heard:
The "Minor Swing" is played, the circle is completed,
The first passion…remembered.

*Now the CD has been replaced by the IPOD. And what next will re-
place the IPOD?

The Silence of Solitude

Through the open window
high in the sky, the full moon
reflects radiance,
a mimicked incandescence
in the deep, deep blue of the night.
No escort now.
No evening star of earlier times.
Solitary,
its transient place
in infinity.

A soft breeze, cooling,
floats in bringing
fragrance of another place, another time,
and the remembrance of his kiss,
that kiss,
his soft beard
seducing a response,
a desire to disappear, dissolve,
effuse into that kiss
and sweet oblivion.

The soft whirr of
the oscillating fan
breaks the moment,
and the silence of solitude.

Deep in the night

Deep in the night
the waters of the river
flow swiftly and silently by,
black, but for the few ripples
reflected from lights on
the twin bridge spans above.
There is little bridge traffic
except for the occasional semi,
disturbing the night's silence,
working through gears
on the inclines.
A faint wind
from the nor'east
brings coolness from
the lake beyond the spans,
and wisps of mist forming.
A front moving in.

From the hazy mist
beneath the spans,
a huge shape emerges,
dark and powerful.
Red and green lights,
port and starboard,
an ore freighter,
low in the water,
at once obtrusive and unobtrusive
to the night's scene.
It comes on in silent power,
gliding like the current,
navigating the river's curve.
From its bridge
a momentary flicker of lights:
reason and ability in control.

Passing,
the thrust
of engines turning giant propellers
deep under the waters,
is felt
more than heard.

Then the freighter is by,
and haze and mist swallow
what might have been
a dream,
an illusion,
now a memory.

A smell of mist and diesel fuel
carried on the night's breeze
is all that remains.
Beyond the spanning bridge,
a faint, faint blush
on the eastern horizon
promises the day to come.

This is the "Blue Water Bridge," over the St. Clair River, at the end of Lake Huron. This bridge joins Port Huron, Michigan, with Sarnia, Ontario. This is where I lived, Port Huron, for a number of years, where my children were born, and raised in their early years, and where I fell in love with sailing and sailed, raced, a beautiful, mahogany, 6 Metre, called "DoDo."

Enticement

Travel south in September,
Down out of the Great Smokies
Where sentinel pines of the piedmont
Greet and invite.

Then there they are…
Fields, acres
Of cosmos:
Pink, purple, and mauve cosmos,

Floating like a fluttering mist
Of shimmering pink chiffon…dancing,
Enticing the eye,
And the spirit.

While above,
Mares' tails
Flick across the
Carolina blue sky.

Fossilized Fish Pantoum

In morning light I view my ancient friends,
Million-year-old fish all fossilized,
With tea and toast, their charm will never end,
They're framed upon my wall to analyze.

Million-year-old fish so fossilized,
One fish swims upstream, the other down,
Framed upon my wall I realize,
The beauty of their lives that I have found.

And where, so long ago, were those fish bound,
Darting here and there in dodging ploy?
Their beauty swimming, just as life was found,
Did they know a sense of fun and joy?

But darting phylogenesis would dodge their ploy,
Did they, of life to come, have some foreseeing?
But since that time sandstone encased their joy,
So had they grasped the wonder of their being?

And now in life today they have a meaning,
With breakfast tea and toast, I comprehend,
The existential wonder of their being,
I view in empathy my ancient friends.

Why Jellyfish?

In DNA technology,
Media tells of the newest advance,
A victimized rhesus monkey egg,
Not given a choice or a chance.

DNA from exotic jellyfish genes,
Injected sans rhesus permission,
Brings forth for scientific amazement (amusement)
An exotic monkey addition.

"ANDI" is his name, the scientists say,
A cute little fellow of curiosity and spark,
And while he resembles his peers as they play,
This ruddy young monkey, glows in the dark.

However…

If into a jellyfish egg, we put monkey DNA matter.
What phenomenon would we then see?
Scary, hairy jellyfish, that patters and chatters,
With the agility to climb up a tree!

Loss

Bright steel of the hatchet flashes an arc,
Cuts through the screeching, to the weathered stump,
Severs the head, lying there now lifeless, as the headless body
Spurting blood, flounders, falls, and flops in the dirt.

At a presumed safe distance, the remaining chickens
Cry low eerie squawks of horror and hysteria,
As the blood-spattered body is taken away:
"We have lost one of our own."

Small groups of people at the harbor's point
Look out to the lake, the stormy, turbid lake,
Where a young man has been washed overboard
From his father's yacht…only son, only child.

Huddled watchers hold their vigil,
Silent voices whisper fears,
Haunted looks, concern, dreading the news:
"We have lost one of our own."

Vincibility

The peacock crows and struts his tail
Through the seasons of the year,
To tempt and tease, all who would watch
His magnificent display.

In stealth the hungry tiger stalks,
But with pounce, the peacock flies,
To the safety of the jacaranda tree,
Hungry tiger loses the day.

When monsoon comes, however, soaking
This audacious feathered array,
To jacaranda tree he can no longer fly,
And on the ground must stay.

With pounce and bounce and slashing flips,
Audacity soon gets eaten.
The tiger licks his smiling lips,
And silently, slinks away.

Promenade

On a lovely May day in Old San Juan's plaza,
They come to perform a daily routine.
She, strictly business, seeks out her own needs,
Then satisfied, flies to the flamboyant tree.

He, however, a discriminating sort,
Decides inspection should rule his day.
So with curiosity, pomp, and pronounced self importance,
He struts his way 'cross mosaic walkways.

Past bright dancing fountains, that cool the warm air,
Past benches, and shoppers who stop to stare,
Daytripping sightseers, and children at play,
With stately aplomb, noting all on his way.

At the end of his grand and regal review,
He comes to the tree where she perches just so,
Satisfied then, away fly the two,
Two comely green parrots of Puerto Rico.

Arias

Among many of Venice's pleasures,
At the waterfront one comes upon,
'Neath colorful awnings that flutter,
A sun dappled market is found.

Fresh seafood and fish from the Adriatic,
Cold-pressed virgin green olive oil,
Vegetables and plants aromatic,
Gastronomical pleasures abound.

Amidst tomatoes and bright green zucchini,
Canaries, in cages so small,
Throats warbling in elated singing,
Outdo hawkers and others around.

Their arias rival Puccini,
Bright melodies filling the air,
Reminiscence of the "Three Tenors,"
A joyous and jubilant sound.

Butterfly
For Julia Butterfly

High, in the sky,
How high, and why?
At the top,
In the tip of the spire
You flit, from branch,
To branch,
Perchance inspire
That many, might stop and think,
And sigh,
That nobility may be passing by,
Nobility, may now surely die,
And you, in innocence, ask…the why
That now, in haste and waste, deny
The reverence of millenniums?

    Enduring dignity could be lost
    To fickle economic cost,
    Greed's power causing dearth.
    Magnifience of eternity
    Erased, so none shall ever see
    The likes again on Earth.

So flit from branch
To tip top branch,
Search for love
In your passionate stance.
Eighteen months
Your treetop dance
Against the moon,
Chrysalis high,
Atop the bright proscenium.

    Vibrant spirit…
    Some of us hear,
    And thank your noble worth.

Self

A statement?
A question?
Noun, or verb?
A reality definable?
A silent anarchistic scream:
    "Look at me!...I am here???"

My children, grown, look to find
Sweet strength,
Warm cookies baked for yet undisciplined egos.
No.
No cloying condescension's to a role unsought here.
I have a public face,
Invisible in crowds,
Masked behind my own closed doors.
So what self then?

On the road, a dead animal, any dead animal,
God bless...
The spontaneous spark of life, there, then gone.
God bless, lost miracle.
My attentions to the tall palm's silhouette,
As dawn's resounding tropical light casts its splendors.
How many colors can I see?
Morning dew sequining a croton's myriad greens...
Joy...
My paints lie quiet...patiently regimented in their drawers.
When will courage come?

With morning, I water the plants,
My tomato plants,
Wondrous...juice, pulp, seeds for forever,
The fruit soon reddening...a blush beginning.

He talks at the table as his food disappears:
"Me! Me!...I! I!"...
"I got the better of him!"
"I got the better of them all!"
"I am! Me! Me!"

"Stop," I say…"Taste the tomato."

"Hummm"…he says
But then quickly again, "I! I! Me! Me!"
And the tomato is no more.
God bless…
And I, too, like the tomato, am forgotten.

With morning, I face my mirror…"sags, lines, spots,
The diminishing spirit fading in the eyes…
"I! I! Me! Me!" is somewhere flying over the Atlantic,
To get the better of "him,"
To get the better of them all.
Soon I must water the plants,
God bless…
And check the lengthening shadows of fall.

In the darkness I open the door.
She is there to greet me,
Her tail a tall question mark.
She demands to be held,
And is on my shoulder rearranging my hair.
In my face,
She says, "Love me."
She searches me for response,
Demanding contentment with her purr.
And contentment comes with my obeisance.

And does self herein lie,
In obedience to expectations?
Neruda said, "I am your dream,
Only that…and that is all."*
God bless…
And if there is no dream,
Do I exist?

*(Excerpt from Love Sonnet LXXXI, by Pablo Neruda)

Bittersweet*

"What are you doing?…"

　　　　　　　　　　"Getting dressed."

"Getting all gussied up
with attitude?"…

　　　　　　　　　　"That's better than going around
　　　　　　　　　　looking grungy."

"Well, somebody's got to do
the work around here"…

　　　　　　　　　　"There are standards to be upheld."

"Whatever"…

　　　　　　　　　　"Do you think he'll"…

"Now don't start that again."

　　　　　　　　　　"But do you?"…

"You know that it wouldn't matter
if you were draped in jewels,
or tarred and feathered,
he wouldn't notice or care"…

　　　　　　　　　　"But his promise"…

"Meaningless"…

　　　　　　　　　　"I know, but it's been so long"…

"Oh, go pet that scrawny cat of yours"

　　　　　　　　　　"Yes, she's the one being in this world
　　　　　　　　　　who truly loves me."

"Damned scrawny bag of bones…
always spitting up on the carpeting"…

　　　　　　　　　　"You're so hard."

"I'm the one who has to clean it up!"…

　　　　　　　　　　…

　　　　　　　　　　"Do you…love me?"…?

…"Of course"…

　　　　　　　　　　"I need you"

"I know."

*This is an exercise to explore possible mental conversations one could
have with oneself, contrasting bitter skepticism with hopeful naïveté.

My Post Menopausal Life

Morning,
Is the best, the most beautiful,
And is lost in all the details
That must be cared for:
Time the eggs, fresh fruit,
Caffeine to get it all started,
Fresh water for the cat,
"You're doing what today?"
A run in my pantyhose,
(Did I forget to take my vitamins?)

The commute.
On 41, I commit the sin
Of driving only five miles over the speed limit.
Agitated male drivers in muscle vehicles
Pass me.
Like frantic sperm, they careen down the highway
Toward their perceived destinations,
And their victory is in getting there.

All day,
I soothe, and pander to
Women such as myself,
Forgotten, neglected, valued only
For required expectations,
Desperate for a little care, attention…
Some recognition,
A gentle touch or embrace…
(True or false, but gentle)…
A soft, honest word,
(Okay…dishonest will suffice)
(Better that than none at all)…
I give them
Much…needed…pampering…

Evening.
Supper prepared,
Dishes washed,
"How was your day" is lost

In television's mediocrity.
Quietly, my Chloe comes to me,
Faithful, more that any other being
Ever in life.
But even she demands attention,
Needs to be petted and stroked,
(As we all do).
But oh, this constant having to give,
Or give way,
Does it ever end?
Or is that the end?
And wherein lies the nobler value?
In adhering to the integrity of convictions?
Or in a grace to submit to life's realities?

When all has been cared for,
Too tired to even brush my teeth,
(Will they fall out in the night?)
I seek solace from my sometimes friend,
The moon,
Who turns her face through the nights
To greet me,
Her glow…
My…gentle caress…
(She asks nothing of me.)

occurrences

Retrospect Friday, September 11, 2001

Hurry, scurry, half thought intentions,
Caught up by…incise
Precise…slice…into awareness.
Numbing shock…realization…
Lacking preparedness for self preservation…
Too late…to negate…this unbelievable…
Inconceivable…

Oh…to turn back time,
Focus attentions…
Change decisions…
Seek preventions…
And act…to hold back…the timeline of fate…
But too late…
And the mangled anguish that twists life…is upon us.

Yates *

She may survive the trial,
She may survive the prison,
Or the mental institution,
But will she survive the dark, cold prison of her own mind?
I cannot judge her.
I have been in that place of constant, overwhelming responsibility.
But I survived, my sweet babes survived,
And their growing, lifelong love for me, is my wonder.

I once had two small gray finches,
Kept in a cage.
One finch was very small,
Quiet, sitting on its perch.
The other, larger, roundly larger,
Jabbering, demanding,
Always demanding,
Domineering.

One morning, I found
A mound of feathers and blood
Spattered on the floor of the cage.
The large, round finch, had been
Pecked and pecked…to pieces,
The small, quiet finch
Sitting on its perch,
Cocked its head, and looked at me.

I took the cage out into the yard,
Opened its door,
And set the little finch free.
It flew up into a tree,
Perched on a branch,
Turned, cocked its head, and looked at me.
And we both knew, it would not survive
The dark, cold prison of the winter to come.
But it had done, what it had done, what it had had to do.

*This concerns a case several years ago of a mother, Andrea Yates, who drowned her babies in a bathtub. At the time of this poem's writing, the case was in the courts once more.

Kursk*

Explosions registered 'round the world,
Submerged and sunk to the ocean's floor,
One hundred eighteen duty bound,
Give everything and more,
Unbearable human cost.
Officials' solemn masquerade,
Steel-willed, faces of stone,
Hide fear of their own incompetence.
And pride overrides possibility,
Contributes to the probability,
That hope is all…but lost…
But hope dives to the ocean's depth.
Hope searches for what could be,
And from the mutilated vessel's hull,
The tapping message comes:
Dot-dot-dot…dash…dash…dash…dot-dot-dot…
Somebody…save…our…souls…help us please…
Dot-dot-dot…save…our…souls…love of God…

As procrastination reigns,
Cold black wetness seeps.
Weakness with each poisoned breath
Surrenders to lasting sleep.
Ultimately darkness
Insinuates its will
Over such courage that remains,
Almost unconscious, still,
The tapping of the haunted heart,
Is felt around the world…
So that through the lone search that is life,
Through the dark night of the sea,
Through layered voices of the gale,
Hear the whispered plea…
Dot-dot-dot…dash…dash…dash…dot-dot-dot…
Love of God…save…our…souls…dot-dot-dot…dot.

*This is about the sinking of the Russian submarine, "Kursk"

Three Mothers

There was a winter bleak not long ago,
Depression deep, caused not by sleet or snow,
Anxiety overwhelmed me to a craze,
Each television screen transfixed my gaze,
As "Desert Storm" ravaged the Middle East,
My mind could find no solace, find no peace.
I'd watch and tears would stream upon my face,
To know my son, could soon be at that place.
My babe, my joy, my noble caring boy:
A victim of a tyrant's cruel ploy?

Remembering childhood, on my way to school,
The symbols of a cherished inducted pool,
Flags on windows, starred for each loved son,
The private devastation of mind and soul
Of mothers bravely trying for self control.

Last night in Alexsinac as missiles flew,
Huddled in her home, a mother too,
Wondered as the bombs burst all around,
Why had life gone mad, and war confound?
She'd taught her son, at breast, and at her knee,
The righteousness of Serbian history,
Of centuries of oppressive persecution,
That ethnic cleansing was the true solution.
And was he now in Kosovo to fulfill,
The promise of the tyrant's vengeful will?

This morning on a hill in Bosnia,
With little feeling left, that of pariah,
Sits cold and wet in snow and mud and sleet,
A mother worn to ultimate defeat.
And when this tragedy had begun,
She'd watched the soldiers take away her son.
And in her heart she knew she'd never see
Again her blessed gift to humanity.
And then the soldiers drove her from her home,
And through miles and miles of mountains did she roam,

With hundreds of her kind all so unwanted,
Their homes usurped, their "right to being" taunted.
And now in vacant, desolate repose,
Her husband, son, are gone, and now she knows
Her younger child too, with her will surely die
In cold and pestilence beneath this sky,
And all she knows to do is wonder why?

And all I know to do is wonder..... Why?

honor,…disgrace,…guilt,…innocence,…
weakness,…strength,…hope,…despair,…
youth,…age,…naïveté,…sage,…
dreams,…schemes,…indolence,…care,…
ambition,……gladness,…joy,…sadness,…
all victims,…of nature's,…indifferent,…madness,…

all,…all,…without a chance,…to plea,…
battered,…and banged,…overwhelmed,…overcome,…
swallowed,…and swirled,…by gigantic,…curl,…
they're washed away, lives gone astray, lives lost this day, to thee
and me,
out,…out to sea,…senselessly,…tsunami…

December 26th, 2004, Southeast Asia

emotions

Decision

When arrogance, bends the rules,
When privilege, right presumes,
When bravado, rules direction,
And incompetence mars ability,
In self-righteous cavalierity,

When reality appears,
Must love blindly self deny,
And acceptingly obey,
Ignoring reason's call,
Refusing to demur,
Sacrificing all?

When is there a point
When reason becomes clear?
When at last to say
That far I will not go,
Not willingly that way.
When does love say no?

The Tiff

It was
Not a demand,
Not a direction,
Merely an extended suggestion
To bridge understanding,
An offered exchange of ideas that was

Overpowered, overwhelmed, by
A verbal violence of temper and ego,
A demanded dominance of even triviality.
About what…?
That which was said?
Or another slight, real or imagined.

The huge porcupine extends,
Expands its quills of self righteous
Indignation,
And supposed wounded feelings,
And is met by…

Silence.
Silence of defense,
Silence in the knowledge of the
    Sanctity in silence,
    Sanity in silence,
    Serenity in silence,
And grace emerges,
    Is grasped at for survival.

The game is so old and overused.
The rift ever deepens.
The gulf between ever widens.
And love is a blinded bird
Silently screeching
In its erratic search for home,
Flying ever farther and farther away.

Legacy of Years

She sits in her chair,
And stares, and hears
The door he has closed as he left.
Moments before?
Or hours?…Or more?…
Or perhaps, even years…
(Does it matter?)

One can tell when someone's connecting,
And too,
One can tell when just fed a line…(a lie.)
But how long has it been since
He's bothered with this…
Not even worth a try.

She sits in her chair and stares…and stares…
At the emptiness life has become:
Conversations slipped 'round one another,
Eyes that do not really meet,
A convoluted equation,
Which lacks the desire to change
This vacuous, lonely connection of lies…
Tragic, oblique evasion.

She sits in her chair, and stares with distrust
Of all that has been so remiss.
Distrust surrounds like a vapor of fear,
Inhaled, evoking regret:
Too much for even one small tear,
Too much to forget.
What loneliness more than this?

And was that you I felt,
    wakening in the still of the night,
    to see the full moon shining down on me,
    and the lagoon beyond, painted in moonlight?

And was that you I felt,
    when the music swelled to
    my trembling core?

And was that you I felt,
    when the sea breeze caressed my cheek,
    filling sails, to balance the hull
    gliding over the swell,
    dancing on waves of green and foam?

And was that you I felt,
    when morning dew
    kissed the flowers
    to colors so vivid my eyes
    could barely behold?

And was that you I felt,
    when dawn's salt air
    filled me with well being?.

How long have I searched for
    you and waited,
    longing for touch,
    and acceptance as I am,
Hoping to find,
Hoping…you'd find…
    but no.
Did we pass one another not knowing?
Did our shadows meet and converse
    in their shadowy way?
Was yours the call unanswered?
Am I guilty of not knowing
    what was,…what is?…
Has it been,…and nevermore?
Insensitivity, at a loss?…

Still…I hope for
    what may be.
Shall continue to wait,
    to search,
    to yearn,
    to say 'til my last breath:
Is that you my love?…

Valentine

Your valentine, today I have received,
To commemorate a love of forty years,
A love at times deceitful, and deceived,
Replete with fears, and jeers, and myriad tears.

But too, a love with hope we sought to capture,
With dreams, and faith, and challenges to face,
Our own created sanctity of rapture,
Through time we danced our sarabande of grace.

With you I've known the best, the worst of times.
You are my heaven/hell both far and near.
And through it all we both have paid our fines,
And still today you are steadfastly here.

So what to you shall now be my reply?
With love and life fulfilled, my sated sigh.

Miss Chloe

Miss Chloe coyly crosses the floor
    on pink, padded paws.
In the far corner she arranges herself,
    tail carefully curls around her feet.
Pink shell ears attune to
    every flutter, every twitch.
Inherent in each movement is her elegance,
    as she turns jewel eyes to

Him across the room, who's any
    enticement she ignores in disdain.
Inherent too, is her instinctively knowing
    what years only have taught me:
Don't trust your soul to that one
    lest it be lost,

Or,
    ignored and forgotten.

After all this time, he still
calls me "Door-is."
My name is "Dar es":
    Dar es Salaam,
The coastal city in Tanzania,
    its meaning being, I could hope
Perhaps my better name:
    "Place of Peace,"

As you my friend have found
    in your far corner.
Would that you
    could have been there,
To give me your wise counsel,
    all those years ago.
But how fortunate I am
    to have it now.

Chloe's Kiss

And I asked myself
"Who would love me?"
"I would," her purr murmurs,
nudging my temple with her small, wet nose,
marking me as her own.

Sappho's influence

Swallows

On a wire in bright morning sunshine singing,
Little swallows chirp with a joyous ringing,
Off they fly an aerial circus winging,
Would I could follow.

How they swoop and dive in such free elation,
Joy of flight for them is life's true sensation,
If I chose a reincarnation station,
I'd be a swallow!

Poetic Self Delusion

How self pleased I am with my lovely poem,
Like a little child with her drawing, calling,
"See, it's for the refrigerator door, once more come
See what I've fashioned!"

Into view a butterfly lightly flying,
Damaged wing, as flutter by, art denying,
Passing, I then utter my question sighing,
Has life less beauty?

latter day drivel

In morning's gentle sunshine
I listen to the CD play:
A young man playing folksongs
On an eight string guitar.
Passion, sensitivity, finesse,
Gently reaching my very core.
Oh, would that I could do something, anything,
So beautifully, so sensitively well.

Well, perhaps, perhaps,
Perhaps loving butterflies, dragonflies,
And the geckos flitting on my path,
The mockingbird's song, the osprey's cry,
The fragrance of jasmine, the morning's sky,
And this guitar's haunting melodies,
Perhaps loving these,
Perhaps I do this loving well.

Whatever has happened, has happened,
    And survives in memory alone.
That, that is to come…we're just guessing.
    Reveries of what could be…are dreams we foment.

The future, the past, are just states of mind,
    And life is to be of this very moment aware,
All joy, peace, fulfillment and care,
    Are there…in this very moment.

So…avow the here and now, as life's greeting…
    Reality, the essence of which is fleeting…
Is a brief, transitional blessing.
    For all there really is…is just this moment…
        this instant…now.

Temptress

Across the seas she comes once more,
    Dancing across the waves and tide,
To the shoreline so appealing,
    To the island's lush seaside,
    And the castle's imposing wall.

She comes in through the open door,
    Across the floor to soar and scurry.
Then up she sweeps to the vaulted ceiling,
    Twirling and swirling, in no hurry,
    Checking out the all and all.

She sings her ancient songs of lore,
    Her moan is low, her sigh is high,
Seducing the air, sensations reeling,
    Temperamental seductress of the sky.
    So, sighing she then sweeps into the hall.

Then with a low seductive roar,
    She causes the prints on the walls to flutter,
And soon she starts to end her dealing,
    She's had enough, and starts to mutter,
    It's time to end this pre-emptive call.

So through the back window she chooses to soar,
    And across the island she once more flies,
Bringing a cool, refreshing feeling
    To all below who search the skies
    To hear this siren's melodies fall.

Across the Atlantic, bye and bye,
    Across the island, to the Caribbean,
What pray tell, is more appealin'
    To the temptress, and her tantrums across the skies?

The Tree

With my morning tea, I look out to see
To see the sea rushing into the shore
Once more, and more, and more,
And more...
Building sands, white sands on the island's shore,
Against coral cliffs.
Winds and waves
Pounding and sculpting,
Sculpting their way, their righteous way,
Again, and again, and again...

And there just above,
Midst jagged rock of the cliff,
Vegetation commences its right to being.
Despite the wild sea, life fights rights to be,
Fights for its own destiny.
And from the confused midst, the bold shape emerges,
The lovely green life of a tree I'm seeing:
Branches uplifted in morning's sunlight,
Sparkling leaves, iridescence, so surges its essence,
In morning's bright
Glorious sight,
Life lifting into the sky.

But, stark reality rules the scene,
Though sparkling with sunlight and radiant green.
A twisted shape is what is seen.
Years and years, and in between,
The winds from the sea, with rhythm and rhyme,
Have pushed and pummeled,
Battered and banged this life I see,
Twisting and turning its destiny,
This convoluted shape before me,
Gnarled and twisted by the winds of time.

And when thought is done
In my mind emerges
The gnarled, twisted shape
Of that which I've become.
Of that once innocence, that was so
Battered, pushed, consoled, yet disillusioned,
By concern, by ego, by emotions, by need,
By power, by ignorance, by arrogance and greed.
By all that fate has thrown at me.
What shape is left?…
What's left of me?…

But looking back now, at the life before me,
At this tree of grace and determination,
I think perhaps I too may show some form of grace,
Some brightness of color, of determination
To stand with some radiance in my place.
And like this tree, it is up to me
In my twisted way, to love life as it comes,
As it comes to me…like the sea…
Like…this tree…

The Expression

Have you heard the expression in spontaneity,
    Casting jest in its singular purview?
One that brings a common hilarity,
    That one could easily misconstrue,
Could be taken with hurt and severity,
        Or taken as so much silly pooh bah,
That something is surely a "too much to-do":
        "As sure as warts on Grandma!"

She fights them of course, the warts you see,
    With potions, and lotions, and exfoliating goo,
And in small pretentions of her own inner dreams,
    She dresses herself in gay favorite hue.
Then out for an outing that seems fancy free,
        Self deceptively driving her illusory landau,
All under control with nothing askew,
        "As sure as warts on Grandma!"

She has seen it all, yet retains dignity,
    Bravely, she won't let decorum unglue,
The future is there like some bright nebulae,
    The sweetness of life, "vie en rose" is her cue,
So life she loves with serene coquetry,
        In glory her story, her last hurrah,
She gives it her all with so much ado,
        "As sure as warts on Grandma!"

With a wrinkle and a twinkle just meant for you,
    She laughs her laugh, her gay tra la la,
With a smile that shines her love so true,
    "As sure as warts on Grandma!"

Anthirium

This floral gift, you present:
A glorious representative of life,
Giant leaves, dark polished green, embrace
Blossoms, springing upwards,
Demanding focus on their grace,
Beauty secured.

From lush swirls, dark red lavish whorls,
Golden stamen's erect anticipation
Of erotic stimulation by
Charmed moth, bee, or fly,
By beauty lured, procured,
In fascination.

So…when velvet fills the evening sky,
And from the whorls of your dark bower
Comes its night blooming flower,
I,
Your butterfly,
Comply.

The Image*

Technology's digital image sends
A message harsh, around the world:
An image, draped and cowering,
Despair, uncomprehending.

Half covered face, offers a glimpse,
Of shattered emotions too intense,
A degradation too immense
For rationality's understanding.

Tears well-up and freely spill
From kohl-trimmed eyes…mesmerize,
Eyes made up to defy abuse,
Cruel misuse, overwhelming degradation.

Despite all strictures, this act defies,
In secrecy, making up these eyes,
Soul's unuttered vow of no compromise,
Infinitesimal hold on self worth.

And though she murmurs not a word,
Mistreatment rife, her psyche numbs,
Her unvoiced statement is felt and heard,
"I am the beauty from whence life comes."

*Several years ago (sometime early in the first decade of the 21st century I think), there was this image of a middle eastern woman, shown and discussed on television, the information media. She may have been Afghani, Iraqi I don't remember, but a woman subjected to the ruthlessness of the religious/political strife going on. This poem was my reaction.

The Brass Ring

A child astride an ornately painted horse
Content with rise and fall around its course
Each rising leap excitement fills the thrill
As down and up the imaginary hill
But voices cry to break the illusory dream
Calling for something more than this, the scream
    "Catch the ring, the ring! That is the thing!"

Disconcerted from the playful rapture
Confused, unknowing, searching a ring to capture
Ah, there it is out there just beyond reach
"Catch the ring!" again is heard the screech
So reaching out the gambler takes a swing
A chance to catch this newly coveted thing
And there it is looped on the tiny finger
So back to mount, there is no time to linger
And looking at this prize newly acquired
A beat up ring of iron that's looking tired
    "No, catch the ring, brass ring! Brass is the thing!"

And so the rider goes around again
Collecting rings each time not knowing then
Forgotten is the faithful painted steed
Forgotten is the dream with this new need
The ride ends and all small hands now hold
Are grubby rings of iron, no brassy gold
And so through life as on and on we go
Collecting grubby rings, somehow we know
Our now forgotten dreams we've set aside
Our search for something more has ruled this ride
And through it all a voice will always call
Just when we think we've finally got it all
    "Catch the ring, the ring! That is the thing!"

Sangria

Brown or red?
The large, domed, oval stone
In the ornate silver ring,
Glows with an inner radiance.
Brown or red?

Lacquered fingertips
Caress its smooth warmth.
She sips red wine and citrus
From blood red Venetian stemware,
And remembers Venice, sparkling Venice.

Flight of pigeons in San Marco,
Shop windows' temptations,
Brown or red?
String after string, like her glowing ring,
Carnelian, jeweled ropes of carnelian.

And the masks, many masks,
Ornate lacquered fascades hiding truths,
As her carefully lacquered maquillage
Hides the realities she keeps to herself,
Hides the soul only she knows.

Fingering her glass, with carnelian clad hands,
Blood red glass, blood red nectar, blood red stone,
Brown or red?
Like the liquid of life surging through her body, her mind,
Enabling memory, and her soul's search for delight.